Heavy Questions

DAVE GRANT RAPS

A Division of G/L Publications
Glendale, California, U.S.A.

© Copyright 1972 by G/L Publications
All rights reserved
Printed in U.S.A.

Published by
Regal Books Division, G/L Publications
Glendale, California 91209, U.S.A.

Library of Congress Catalog Card No. 78-185800
ISBN 0-8307-0112-5

Contents

Dear Dave,

You have written a book that really answers, without compromise and with real common sense, the questions young people are asking. You relate to them on their level, with love, with truth, with firm conviction.

As I travel back and forth across this country, I meet a lot of young people who are searching, wondering, wanting to know the truth. They see rules and regulations and unhappy people. They see friends who are being transformed and who are excited about Jesus Christ. These two groups advocate the same thing—Christianity. No wonder people are asking questions!

HEAVY QUESTIONS is for those who are searching for fresh, sound answers.
HEAVY QUESTIONS is for those who have recently found Christ, who still have questions about their new life.
HEAVY QUESTIONS is for those who love young people and want to lead them to Christ.

I am thankful that Christianity is becoming so much more relevant to youth, Dave. Through men like you many more young people will see the relevance of Christ and the need for Him in their lives. I trust that everyone who reads this book will be drawn closer to the Saviour and His way of living!

Sincerely,

Nicky Cruz
Founder and President
Outreach, Inc.

ABOUT RELIGION

Isn't one religion as good as another?

Very possibly, yes. It is also possible that one religion is as bad as another. This would be based on the premise, "No milk is better than poison milk." It may be that no religion is better than the wrong one. My experience has been that religious people are the most difficult to reach with the truth. Too often their minds are like concrete: all mixed up and permanently set!

The question is not how good or truthful other religions are. The fact is that man is desperately in need of the divine redemptive act that took place at Calvary. The cross of Jesus Christ has no counterpart in religion. Man doesn't need a religion; he needs a relationship.

How do you
define religion?

As most people think of religion today, I would define it as man's best effort to find God. (In most cases he will be honest enough to admit he hasn't.) With religion, the initiative is with man. However, the relationship that man needs is initiated by God. It is God's effort to reach man. Religion is a quest of the abstract. True Christian faith is a communion with the personal. Religion is a shot in the arm to ease the pain. What man needs is an operation.

What do you think of the statement, "Religion is the opiate of the people"?

I think it is basically true. Opiate is a drug and its effect is to dull the senses. I think history points out that the most religious nations are the most godless. The more religion they have, the more they seem to be steeped in darkness, fear, ignorance and superstition. In John 8:32 it says, "You shall know the truth, and the truth shall make you free." If the majority of the world is religious but not free, what does that tell you?

What's Satan's attitude toward religion?

I think he's all for it. It's possible that religion is Satan's "ace trump," so to speak. He doesn't care how religious you are. You can be baptized, catechized, confirmed, Bar Mitzvahed or whatever. He would like all of that if it would distract you from the *real issue*—the surrender of your will to Jesus Christ!

What do you say when
a person tries to
tell you that religion
is a crutch?

Agree. For many people religion is something you use when in a jam or in need. Religion has often been compared to a parachute: something you have, but hope you'll never have to use. Beyond religion there is a relationship. Just as man has an absolute need for breathing in the physical, he has the same need spiritually. You could hardly accuse people who breathe as using their lungs as a crutch.

You said that
Christianity is
the only way.
I think that's
narrow. Isn't
it perhaps the
best way?

If the Christian faith is not the only way (John 14:6) then it's the worst way. It makes too many fantastic claims and promises that it couldn't possibly deliver such as hope, forgiveness, eternal life, unless Christ is real.

What is the sustaining
force of religion?

Fear.

My experience with religion of nearly every label has been that it is motivated and sustained by fear. I can't prove it but I am of the opinion that if we could take from religion the element of fear it would cease to exist. Let's keep this in perspective by this consideration. Many a person has come to God *because* of fear—fear of death, punishment and the unknown.

But at the moment a person truly encounters the power of God with the overwhelming confidence of forgiveness and hope, his life is motivated and sustained by love.

The Apostle Paul said, "For the love of Christ controls and urges and impels us . . ." (2 Corinthians 5:14 *Amplified*).

I'm sick and
tired of religion
being forced down
my throat.

I don't blame you. Many people try to force religion usually with great pain and little results. Try to forget your religious regurgitations and remember that nobody, but nobody can force you to love God and love your neighbor. But when you willingly choose to love you will be well on your way. Of course, the opposite is also true. No matter how religious you are, if you fail to love God and neighbor, your life is a total failure because that's what life is all about.

DATING AND SEX

What do you think
about young people
going steady?

Most young people go steady not because of love, but for social security. There is a need to be accepted and belong to someone.

An advantage of going steady is you find a degree of that security. The guy doesn't have to worry about making the big impression on a different girl each weekend. If he dates a lot, going steady is less expensive. The girl doesn't have to sit by the phone wondering if anybody loves her. She knows that for any social occasion she has some-one to be with.

Are there any
disadvantages
of going steady?

The disadvantages are: it tends to be a selfish relationship ("you're mine") that leads to jealousy if there is any breach of understanding. Contrary to some opinions, love is not jealous.

Going steady obviously leads to a more familiar relationship. Becoming more familiar, we relax and barriers begin to dissolve. A familiar situation (even for Christians) has too often led to unintentional compromise. Just because you're a Christian doesn't mean your glands have gone out of gear!

what eventually
happens to most
of these relationships?

They split. And when they split it's usually obvious they didn't love each other because of the way they treat and talk about each other. People who love don't seek to destroy those with whom they have had disagreements or a parting-of-the-ways.

The wrong attitude in these relationships creates what is known as the predatory male and the spoiled female. The male exploits the girl sexually and the female exploits the boy financially. It develops into a very bad habit that too often is carried over into the marriage.

Sex is natural.
Why fight it?

So is fire. Controlled it provides light and warmth. Uncontrolled it ravages and destroys. Can we trust our conscience or emotions? How often has a glandular whim mocked self-control. Sex is best enjoyed within the secure bonds of a total union, physical, emotional, social, legal. A good lasting relationship needs all the help it can get. Careless, undisciplined sex is not a good cohesive. The physical dimension of sex should be the completion of your union, not the initiation.

What do you think about pre-marital sex?

What this question usually means is, "What do you think about sexual intercourse prior to the wedding?" If we define a couple of words it may help us in our answer.

The word marital is from the same word as marriage; it means union. Now the question reads, "What do you think of pre-union union" and there isn't any such thing! The real question should be, "How married can you get?"

If you're asking, "How far can we go . . . ?", you're on the wrong track. You should be asking, "What does love require?"

What do you think about trial marriages?

The argument is, "You need experience before making a commitment." They say "You wouldn't buy a pair of shoes before trying them on, would you?"

One answer might be: I'd rather buy a pair without trying them on than get caught with a pair worn by everyone in town. When people speak of experience they usually mean the physical act of sexual intercourse. Even if you proved you were biologically compatible, this would hardly be the basis for a good and lasting relationship.

Oftentimes the argument for experience is that it will avoid a bad honeymoon. If you're going to have a bad experience, it would be far better that you have it within the bonds of trust, patience, tenderness and the confidence of tomorrow than in the wham-bam, furtive, insecure testing ground of some guy's launching pad.

what do you
think about sex
education in
school?

Let's start with the premise that sex education is necessary from somewhere. If not school, what are the options? Ideally, the education should come from parents in the home. But most statistics prove otherwise. If not home, where? Do you get this information from church, parish or synagogue? Very seldom. About the only option left is friends and/or enemies more commonly known as the street.

Personally, if my only option was school or the street, I'd pick the school. Equally important is the next question.

What do I say to a professor who says about sex, "You need experience before marriage"?

After class, go up to his desk and ask him to introduce you to his daughter.

What is
sex education?

Sex education is a combination of information (or facts, not necessarily true) and attitude. The right facts are certainly necessary, but hardly solve the problem. We should read the books and be aware of all the anatomical apparatus. But attitude is just as important. If you have the wrong attitude (and that can be either extreme—prude or playboy) toward the right information, you're no better off than when you were ignorant.

The best attitude begins with respect for your own humanity. This is reflected in your consideration of the opposite sex. Is he a thing to be used, or someone created in the image of God?

What would you say is
the result of fornication?
A large number of teenagers
are holding the view that
premarital sexual intercourse
is as innocent as a
goodnight kiss.

If sexual intercourse is as innocent as kissing, why don't people get pregnant from kissing?

Do you think the
New Morality is
valid?

Here again, we had best begin by definition. I don't think that "true" morality is ever new. Morality based on principle is changeless. Whereas moral behavior determined by tradition, edicts, mores and regulations does need and require a continuing re-evaluation.

The main weakness of the popular "New Morality" is that it has grossly underestimated human nature and equated love with "what I feel is right." To say that love makes it right sounds good, but it's unrealistic. You can love the wrong thing. 1 John 2:15 says: "Love not the world . . ." 1 Timothy 6:10 states: "The love of money is the root of all evil."

Sometimes morality can be determined by the situation. The determining factor is not the thing itself, but the situation or usage. Sex is neither right nor wrong. The question is, what situation or misuse of sex makes it adultery?

FACT: I took a package out of a store.
SITUATION: I paid for it—that's "good."
SITUATION: I didn't pay for it—I'm in trouble!

How do you help
a homosexual?

The same way you help anyone else with a problem. They must recognize they have a problem and want help. The secret is in admitting what you are—not what you do. Very few homosexuals will admit they have a problem or need; therefore, they cannot be helped. Anyone, homosexual, gambler, alcoholic, who honestly admits his need and sincerely seeks assistance can be helped.

I have a girl friend who has led a really bad life. I mean, she has done everything in the book and then some. She has asked me, "Will God forgive me and after washing away my past and giving me a bright future, can I again say I'm a virgin?" I honestly don't know what to tell her.

You can tell her that her bad life is really not the problem. What she should be concerned with is her relationship with God. It's too easy to go after the problem backwards by dealing with the symptoms, rather than the cause.

It would be a very frustrating and fruitless experience if you were to try sweeping all the darkness out of a room before turning on the light. Turn on the light! The light will take care of the darkness.

And, no, she can't say she's a virgin for reasons that should be obvious. Forgiveness is spiritual not physical. Here's a parallel example that might help: God can give a man the strength to overcome alcoholism, but the man might still have to live out his life with a bad liver.

what do you think
about marriage
across religion
lines?

First of all you need to make a distinction between a religion and a denomination. A marriage between a Roman Catholic and a Jew is one thing. A marriage between a Presbyterian and a Methodist is something else. There can, of course, be broad differences between denominations such as when one is a strong Calvinist and the other a strong Arminian.

In a day of considerable tolerance it is not quite the problem it has been. But then, tolerance is not a virtue if you don't believe anything.

What you ultimately must decide is whether the two of you walk in the light. The Bible asks the question: "What communion has light with darkness?"

How come
parents are
always telling
or trying to
influence you,
what boy
to like?

Since I don't know your parents, let me give you several possibilities and see if you can figure it out.

(1) They think they know what's best.
(2) They are very status conscious and want you to do well.
(3) Because of some boys you've liked in the past, they don't trust your judgment.
(4) They may be getting some pressure from his parents.
(5) They love you very much and wish to give you guidance in what could lead up to the biggest decision of your life.

My parents don't trust me, what should I do?

Why don't they trust you? Look at the problem from another angle. Who do you trust? Aren't they the ones who've proved to you they can be trusted? You trust him (or her) because they've earned that trust by performance.

Act responsibly in little things as well as big things and chances are good you'll be treated the same. (Important note—especially to parents: We are influenced in life by people who believe in us, not by those in whom we believe.)

JUDGMENT AND HELL

How can a God of love
send anybody to hell?

That question is similar to, "When are you going to stop beating your wife?" It's a non sequitur. God doesn't send anybody anywhere. The Bible says, "God is not willing that any should perish . . ." Our struggle is that of the "will". My will, or God's will. What do I want? If I will not say to God now, "Thy will be done," he has no other alternative but to say to me on the day of judgment, "All right, David, *thy* will be done!" In hell every man finally gets what he wants; he gets himself!

It is his choice. The wrath of God is not an emotion; it's a consequence. The real question is: How can a God of justice allow anyone to go to heaven? What right do you have to go to heaven? None. Can you imagine what it would be like in heaven as people sat around discussing how they got there? (Turn your imagination loose with that for a while.) If I could do one thing to get to heaven, for all eternity you'd never hear the end of it! Any and all will be there for the same reason: the mercy and grace of the Lord Jesus Christ. Period.

I've always thought
I would go to hell
if I do bad things.

Not true. If we concede that there is nothing good you can do to get to heaven (Ephesians 2:8,9), then the opposite is also true; you don't go to hell because of bad things. If you are saved because of faith, then you are lost because of lack of faith. Again the issue is a relationship. "He that has the Son has life; he that has not the Son of God has not life" (1 John 5:12).

What will happen to those who have never heard about Jesus Christ?

From the recorded history we have, we know that man has always been saved by faith. From God's eternal perspective there is no point in history when Christ died. "He was slain before the foundation of the world" (1 Peter 1:20). We may be assured that no man can be saved apart from what Christ did. The best way to really answer this question is in light of God's character. God is just. Genesis 18:25b asks the question, "Shall not the Judge of all the earth do right?" Whatever God does with you, or anyone else, will be right.

Do christians
face judgment?

Yes, but perhaps not in the way you think. All men will be judged, but there are two judgments: One for believers and one for unbelievers.

The unbeliever faces the Great White Throne. (See Revelation 20:11–15.) The record of men in the areas of faith and conduct will be read. No appeal will be heard, no excuses tolerated, no mitigating circumstances presented. The issue is life and death. "He who believes in the Son has eternal life; he who does not obey the Son shall not see life, but the wrath of God rests upon him." (John 3:36 *RSV*).

Regarding the believer, Paul declares: "For we must all appear before the judgment seat of Christ; that everyone may receive the things done in his body, according to that he has done, whether it be good or bad" (2 Corinthians 5:10). Here the issue is rewards, not life or death.

The unbeliever's judgment is faith. The believer's judgment is works. The rewards are determined by the materials with which we have structured our lives.

What difference does it make if I don't believe in Jesus Christ?

It makes a hell of a difference!

BELIEVING

What did you mean, "There's a God-shaped vacuum in every man?"

You were created by God—to have union and fellowship with Him. That union was broken by Adam with the results being death. We call that broken union sin. If you die without renewing that union, it's called hell. The only way God has provided for bringing man back into fellowship with God is by his act of love on the cross.

Without God you are incomplete, there is something missing, an emptiness, a vacuum. We try to fill that void with everything imaginable such as money, pleasure, sex, success and education. These just don't meet the real need. I think St. Augustine said it very well: "Man's heart strives after unending eternal happiness. Thou hast created us, O Lord, for Thyself and our heart is restless until it rests in Thee."

Do you believe
our future is
predestined ?

The only predestined person is Jesus Christ. If you are united with His life, you share His predestination. God knows your life from beginning to end. From your human viewpoint it might seem as if your life were predestined. But you must remember that with God there is no future—only now.

My parents are afraid
I'll lose my faith if I
go to a secular college –
what do you think?

That would depend on how strong your faith is. It takes great faith to be able to doubt. There are some things you should consider. First, getting a lot of information doesn't mean you've discovered truth. How much of what we know is truth? Will Rogers said, "All men are ignorant, just on different subjects!" The more you learn, the more you realize you don't know. Secondly, don't separate knowledge between the sacred and the secular. *All* knowledge (regardless of its label— science, philosophy, math, music) that is truth is of God and is sacred. God determined every true law and principle that you will ever study.

Then, too, consider those who teach. There are basically two kinds of professors: the Wreckers and the Builders. Anyone (even a child) can tear them down. Respect a teacher for the discipline of his learning but remember that a Ph.D. behind his name doesn't mean he can speak *ex cathedra* on every other subject.

I read in a gossip column once that a person believed that the Ten Commandments were made to prove that people weren't perfect. Is this true? If so, why have I always heard that they were a set of laws? If this isn't true, how would you convince this person that there are a set of laws?

They are a set of laws whose ultimate achievement has been to show us we can't keep them. A mirror is not made to wash your face, but it does show you what you look like. The Ten Commandments show up our badness. Jesus said, "If you break one, you're guilty of all." That means everybody has missed it. The next question then should be, "What do I do now?" Admit that you haven't and can't live by the rules. Then accept the fact that God has forgiven you and will accept you because of what Christ has done for you.

How does religious persecution affect the Christian faith?

On a collective, organized basis it might be put out of business or be driven underground. But on the level of personal commitment it should have no effect. When we think of religious repression we visualize laws against religious services, no opportunity to buy or read Bibles in public and even some atheist getting a law passed so we can't have public prayer in schools.

The mark of a believer is love. You can't legislate love out of people's lives. By the way, do you have any idea how most Christians responded to the professional atheist who was responsible for getting public prayers out of schools?

Their reaction was typically religious, but hardly that of love and compassion.

How does the Christian conversion meet my psychological need like nothing else does?

It does so in many ways but primarily by bringing a balance between our "two natures." We have a need for self-criticism and a need for self-acceptance. We have a simultaneous need for both and nothing can give you that except a right relationship with God.

Some go overboard on self-criticism: "I'm no good—I'm a terrible sinner, a lowly worm." They can find nothing good in or about themselves. They're out of balance. The other extreme is on self-acceptance, or self-righteousness, summed up by the Pharisees' pious proclamation, "I thank my God I am not as other men!"

When you put these two together you find a beautiful balance that comes out like this:
"I am a sinner———
———and a child of God!"

Do you think most
people believe
in God?

According to most polls, somewhere between 90–95% of the American population profess to believe in God. However, I think it would be more accurate to say that this percentage believes there *is* something—love? truth? LIGHT? FIRST cause? Call it God. They do not believe in a personal relationship with a living reality.

I *believe* there *are* witches, demons, ouija boards, and horoscopes. But I don't believe *in* them. I don't trust them. I don't follow them. I won't commit my will and life to them.

There is an eternity of difference between believing there *is* and believing *in*.

By the way, the answer is No.

You said you
didn't like the
word "christian."
why?

It is so badly misunderstood. It means so many things to so many people. To some it means "gentile." To others it is synonymous with Roman Catholic. It is not uncommon for people to think, if you're born in America, you're a Christian. This confusion comes from lack of separation of church and state in most countries. Certain nations are thought of as Muslim, Hindu or Christian.

Our relationship with God is not determined by where we are born. It is determined by our relationship and our personal response to His love as ultimately expressed by the death and resurrection of Jesus Christ.

Perhaps the most accurate word to use would be "believer" or "unbeliever."

People in heaven
are good, not bad.
You said bad!
Explain!

The only goodness that God recognizes is that of Jesus Christ. The Bible says that all of our righteous deeds are like polluted garments. (See Isaiah 64:6.) If I must be good to enter heaven, I never will. People in heaven are bad in the sense they have recognized and admitted their best is not enough. Hell will be entered into by those who considered themselves good, moral and law-abiding. (Read Luke 18:9-14.) The only ones to spend eternity in the presence of God will be those who have admitted their own badness and trust in the goodness provided by Jesus Christ.

What's the difference
between an atheist and
an agnostic?

An atheist is one who believes there is no God, or Supreme Being. An agnostic is a person who thinks it is impossible to know whether there is a God.

An atheist must almost claim to be omniscient. That is, to have studied far and wide and to have discovered no proof whatsoever of a Supreme Being. If you have a friend who claims to be an atheist, you might ask him, "Have you been everywhere?" "No." "Do you know everything?" "No." "Is it possible that God exists in some area about which you know nothing?" If he's honest, he must answer, "Yes." He's now an agnostic.

Are either of
these related
to idolatry?

It is interesting that the Bible doesn't really deal with either atheism or agnosticism. The closest it seems to come is Psalm 14:1: "The fool says in his heart, 'There is no God'."

Idolatry is another matter of grave concern. God has put within every man the need and desire to worship. Therefore, we may assume that every one worships something, if nothing more than bowing at the shrine of his own ego.

Idolatry is the worship of the creature rather than the Creator. (See Acts 17:22–31 and Romans 1:25.) You are a slave to that which you worship. You can be no bigger than your god. And when you worship a cow (snake, rabbit, monkey, money, pleasure, whatever) what can you expect?

I had a teacher who said, "It doesn't matter what you believe, if you believe sincerely."

Ask him if he's talking about Hitler!! You can't divorce belief and behavior. A good life does not proceed from an evil principle.

The law says you can think what you like as long as you don't transfer it into deeds. The song says, "you can't go to jail for what you're thinking."

The Bible says, "For out of the heart proceed evil thoughts, murders, adulteries, fornications, thefts, false witness, blasphemies" (Matthew 15:19).

You can't get clear water from a dirty stream. If a man is not held responsible for what he believes, then how can he be held responsible for how he believes?

What do you mean
by "most confessions
are meaningless"?

Too often people are confessing or admitting the wrong thing. They hear a sermon and are convicted of something they've done or are doing. So they confess a long list of things and go away feeling better. They confuse the "feeling" with resolving the issue with God.

If you are an unbeliever, the *only* thing to confess is what you *are*—a sinner, a rebel—one who has lived his life apart from God. It would be much easier to confess what you have *done,* but it wouldn't solve your problem.

When you have confessed or admitted your state of living for self and are converted to the state of living for God, then and only then do the things you do (sins) become the issue. (See 1 John 1:9.) (You might also check the story of the Pharisee and the Publican found in Luke 18.)

HYPOCRISY

I am tired of the
hypocrisy of church
members. I feel
that I am just
as good as they are.

It is very possible that you are. However, church members don't happen to be the criterion of goodness. Seeking that kind of justification is like saying, "I'm just as free as any slave." The Bible doesn't say that all have sinned and come short of the glory of the church members. Comparing your goodness to Jesus Christ is quite another story.

All we have is a bunch of cackling turkeys at this church and I'm getting sick of it. They won't even put themselves out for these kids, so the teens have to do it. How can we change this church?

Love them to death!

What is sin?

Sin is not lying, stealing, cheating, getting drunk or running around with women! All of these items, plus at least 100 more, are the results of sin. They are merely symptoms of the problem. For instance, stealing a horse doesn't make you a horse thief. You steal a horse because you are a horse thief. Sin is not what I do; it is what I am. It is a state of being, a separation from God who is truth, love and light. If in your lifetime you fail to accept Christ, who is the bridge over that gap, you are eternally separated from God, and that's hell! Literally. And this, of course, answers the question: What does "the wages of sin is death" mean?

If someone is sincere and does his best, isn't that enough to get him do heaven?

No. You can be sincerely wrong. The Bible says that your very best, compared with what God demands, is really a lot of dirty rags. (See Isaiah 64:6.) The Pharisees were very good, religious, law-abiding men. But Jesus said, "That except your righteousness shall exceed the righteousness of the scribes and Pharisees, ye shall in no case enter into the kingdom of heaven" (Matthew 5:20). Doing your best is not only not enough—it isn't even the issue.

Is there such
a thing as one sin
being worse than
another in God's eyes?

From God's viewpoint the answer is, no. Because that which separates us from God is not degrees of what we do, but the absolute of what we are. From the human or horizontal dimension, one sin or wrong can be worse than another because of the social consequences.

You talked about
man's sinful
nature; don't
you think that
man is
naturally good?

No. Man is by nature selfish and self-centered. I don't know of anyone who has ever drifted into virtue. But even if you could make yourself a good person, it wouldn't solve the problem. Being a sinner doesn't mean you are bad, it means you are living a life separated from God. You can be a good sinner or a bad sinner, a moral or an immoral sinner. Again, the main issue is in the being, not the doing.

SIN

When I go to school and attend my Christian youth club, I know the kids who run the club. Later in the day I'll see these same kids doing things I know very well a Christian wouldn't do. I find this true wherever I go, including church. This doesn't help us kids one bit as far as making a choice for Jesus is concerned. What are we supposed to think of this?

I would like to give you at least three things to think about:

(1) Other people should not and cannot be the standard by which we measure our lives.
(2) "Judge not, that you be not judged. For with the judgment you pronounce you will be judged, and the measure you give will be the measure you get. Why do you see the speck that is in your brother's eye, but do not notice the log that is in your own eye?" (Matthew 7:1–3).
(3) If you observe something you wouldn't do, then be sure you don't.

How can you be
a good christian
in the crowd?

Your question will be easier to answer if I can change your word good to strong. If you are a strong Christian, you can go around any crowd. If you are weak or immature, you cannot.

When you are strong, you are insulated—not isolated. Jesus Christ did not live in an ivory tower separated from the world. One of the biggest complaints of the religious people was that he was the friend of publicans and sinners. If you are not strong, you need spiritual isolation and protection, just as a baby that is weak and immature needs protection from the crowd.

What is the best way
to approach a teen-
ager on the subject
of Christ? They are
so indifferent.

Live your life in such a manner (love, joy, peace, the "natural" high of the Spirit) that they can't help noticing the difference. Live your life in such a way that if God did not exist, it wouldn't make sense! In a day of synthetics and facades, that kind of reality will overcome their indifference.

In trying to justify their behavior, some of my friends have tried to convince me that sin is relative. Is it?

That would depend a lot on the definition of sin. If by sin they mean goods and bads, rights and wrongs, traditions, mores or cultural conditioning, then the answer is yes. If by sin they mean "the transgression of the law," that "law" being to love God and love one another, the answer is no. In all the world I've never met two people who would agree on what we ought to do or not do. But I think all men everywhere agree on what we ought to be. That's where we must begin.

You said there
are no bad
words. Please
explain.

Too often we lump all so-called bad words in the same category. We fail to distinguish between swearing, profanity, blasphemy, obscenity and vulgarity, all of which are really neutral. It is possible to use almost any word in a good or bad way. We are conditioned to words being bad. Is there really any difference in dog or bitch, illegitimate or bastard? No. They mean the same. They become bad because of their usage. Words are only vehicles to express our thoughts and feelings. ". . . for out of the abundance of the heart, the mouth speaks" (Matthew 12:34).

You said, "There are no bad words." You've got to be kidding!

If you will check the origin of the word *kidding,* you will find it began as a vulgar expression. No word, of itself, is bad, but you can use almost any word in a bad manner. Swearing, profanity, vulgarity and blasphemy are all the bad usage of words. Many words are considered inappropriate in some situations and groups of people.

We usually use words we consider bad to demean or dehumanize another person. The problem is why you feel it necessary to express contempt, not the words you have chosen. I don't tell anyone to go to hell because it's not my prerogative. There's nothing bad in the word hell. If you were breeding dogs no one would question your use of the word bitch. But using it to question someone's heritage is something else.

Be careful you don't have a double standard and stand in judgment on people who use words outside your frame of conditioning. Of course, a little self-control never hurt anyone.

If I stub my toe
and say "crunch" or
"peanut butter" or
"heck" or "?" and
it makes me feel
better, is this wrong?

No! It's great if you can have that kind of controlled release on your emotions.

DRUGS

Why do adults
get so uptight
about drugs when
they have worse
problems?

They may be genuinely concerned and again they may be using it as a smoke screen. Most of us seek to justify by comparison. "Marijuana is no worse than alcohol, therefore . . ." If strychnine were no worse than arsenic, would it be safe? Of course not! Every element must stand or fall alone. Each of us should be willing to admit and deal with his own problem. When the Bible says my "body is the temple of the Holy Spirit," that covers the use of drugs, alcohol, gluttony and proper rest.

Do you think it's wrong to experiment with drugs?

It all depends. Under the controlled supervision of a doctor it could be very rewarding. Experimenting under the pressure of a dare or group acceptance could be dangerous. What if I told you I had discovered a new chemical additive for cars. You put this chemical in your car and it will do things you never dreamed of. It will take the wildest trip imaginable. But I must be honest and warn you that it's unpredictable, it may be only able to take a couple of trips before something blows. Would you be willing to experiment with this chemical in your car? I would imagine your response would be, "Of course not. Do you think I'm stupid?" I don't know, are you?

How much is your car worth?

How much is your brain worth?

Since marijuana is not as bad as alcohol, why shouldn't it be legalized?

Arguing to legalize a lesser problem is almost like the fellow who has one disease, so figures another one won't hurt. As of this writing, there simply isn't enough known about the long-range effects of regular smoking of marijuana. If after a number of years of testing it does indeed prove relatively harmless, it may be legalized.

Once society is involved in a problem there is seldom an easy solution. Recently in New York City there was a special drive to dry up the source of drugs. It was fairly successful. The supply became very low. Consequently the price skyrocketed on what was available. The result of this was the skyrocketing of crime, primarily robberies, to pay the price. So what do you do? Choose the lesser of two evils?

THE CHRISTIAN LIFE

When you meet a
person you dislike
or can't stand,
should you put on
a front and be nice,
or what?

Jesus said, "Love your enemies, and pray for those who persecute you . . ." (Matthew 5:44). Ask yourself this question: "If I knew I loved the person, how would I treat him?" Having determined that, treat him that way regardless of how you feel. The Christian thing to do is always the right thing to do, regardless.

Do you think
daily devotions
really do any
good?

If they are not mechanical in the sense of "duty," a quiet time with God will do at least three things:

(1) Stabilize your life. Your conversion is your new *foundation*. Visualize your life as a tall TV tower. It is set firmly on the foundation. Then you attach guy wires in several directions in order to give it stability. This allows the tower to bend with the wind and not break.

(2) Preparation. In a real sense life is a battle or contest. Putting on a uniform and carrying a weapon won't win the war. There must be pre-combat strategy and training. When David was confronted with a bear, and a lion and then a giant, he didn't have time for a committee session or an all-night prayer meeting. His daily preparation made him ready for the time of testing. Proper preparation not only provides victory it eliminates many battles in advance.

(3) You will be in a position to know God's will. "The steps of a good man are ordered by the Lord" (Psalm 37:23). I do not know the way I shall go, but well do I know my Guide.

should I feel
guilty if I'm a
believer in Jesus
Christ and don't
witness?

It is impossible to be a believer in Christ and not *be* a witness. Witness is a noun, not a verb. It is what I *am* more than something I do. When I profess to be a follower of Jesus Christ I am marked. The Bible tells us that when God's Spirit indwells us we will be His witnesses. The world will know we are His followers by our love. When our lives demonstrate this love we may be assured we will have ample opportunity to make "witness" a verb and share our experience.

Unfortunately, there isn't a law against impersonating a "Christian."

Would you comment on freedom?

Freedom is two-dimensional. One side is choice; the other is responsibility. We've gone to an extreme that sounds like a broken record: "I've got my rights." I've got a right to swing my arm. It's my arm. But my "freedom" ends where your nose begins. And if I don't accept that responsibility, I forfeit my "right."

Freedom is not the right to do as I please; it's the privilege to do as I ought. Every day there is a new legislation "forcing" us to do things we ought to have done when we had the chance to exercise our freedom.

In 1 Corinthians 13 we are reminded that "Love does not insist on its own rights or its own way." Freedom must always be exercised in conformity to the higher "law" of love.

I want to be a
professional soldier.
Now, how would that
apply to Christ?

It would be determined by why you want to be a professional soldier. If you desire to be a professional soldier in order to have a legitimate reason to bully or to kill people, you have a serious problem. If, on the other hand, you desire the discipline and rigorous life of a professional soldier, it could be very healthy.

Can a person be a
Christian and go to
war?

Yes. But let's look a little closer at the definition of war and its causes. Even the best of friends have differences of opinion causing conflict. That's war.

A gang or group of criminals moves in on new turf. They try to take over a business or territory. That's war. What is it that makes them want to gain for themselves at the expense of others? What flaw in human nature compels an individual in this direction?

If nothing were inherently wrong with man's nature, we would never need protection or law enforcement. You can be at "war" with a person all your life and never touch them. There is conflict and tension between people in every area and level of life.

We usually think of a war on a massive scale. The cause of war between masses is the same as two people arguing over a property line. To take a man's life by violence is never a priority solution.

As bad as death seems, it is not the ultimate evil. To live for a hundred years and never experience God's love is far worse.

What do you
give up as a
Christian?

On the social level, you give up nothing. When you accept Christ into your life, he simply gives you a higher set of values. Many things you considered important are suddenly insignificant. "He is no fool who gives what he cannot keep to gain what he cannot lose." Jim Elliot. I would like to make a slight change to your question and answer it again. . . .

what do you give
up to become a
christian?

The toughest thing in the world—yourself! "For whoever would save his life will lose it, and whoever loses his life for my sake will find it" (Matthew 16:25).

What's so wrong with cheating if no one gets hurt?

Can you guarantee that? (The excuse I like better than that one is, "You've got to cheat to keep up with the cheaters.") How would you like to be operated on by a doctor who cheated on his exams? I think the Golden Rule should eliminate most cheating: Do unto others as you would have others do unto you. The one who's always hurt by cheating is the cheater. You're probably familiar with the truism, "There's no honor among thieves." Why? A thief doesn't trust himself so he doesn't trust anyone. One who continually cheats doesn't trust himself. The consequences? Everyone is suspect. That seems a high price for a short-cut. If you accept the premise that cheating is only wrong when someone is hurt, then it should always be wrong.

AND OTHER
EVERYDAY THINGS

When it comes to certain social involvements, how can I reply to "How will you know if you don't try it?"

Experience is not always necessary for either knowledge or understanding. I doubt if anyone would propose that question to a doctor treating a serious disease. By careful study and observation he knows the cause, effects and cure without ever experiencing the disease. It ought to be obvious you don't have to be bitten by a rattlesnake to know what poison is.

What do you
think of capital
punishment?

Capital punishment is similar to the "wrath of God" i.e., it is a consequential event. Society, of which we are all a part, sets up laws and guidelines to protect itself. If I am aware of those laws and the consequences of breaking them, then I am responsible for bringing down the "wrath" on my own head.

Society punishes its members by taking away one or both of the things we cherish most, time and money. If you can't give money, you pay with time. In a real sense time and life are the same. We usually measure life by duration rather than quality. The greater the offense, the more time (life) is taken away. For the ultimate offense; society takes all of some one's time. The consequence being the guilty party forfeits all of his time (life) either instantly or for its duration. The termination of man's life (time) is not the ultimate evil. In understanding God's purpose for life (to love Him and one another) the ultimate tragedy is not the termination of time, but a fully extended time that is wasted or unfulfilled. I believe capital punishment is a viable principle, but it has been unfairly used. As long as mainly the poor die, it is unfair, but this does not negate the principle.

WHY DO SO MANY
PEOPLE SEEM TO
BE LOOKING FOR
ESCAPE ?

Escape, in and of itself, is not a "bad" thing. All our life there will be times when we need to "get away" just for rest and change. That's when we need to put our minds and bodies into neutral. Even God "got away" on the seventh day!

If you are trying to *run away* from life or even yourself, that's something else.

In all of man's history there have been those who sought escape by means of drink, drugs and different forms of isolation. Insanity is a form of mental withdrawal—or escape. We must learn to handle stress and conflict. Just as we *increase* our physical capacity by putting stress on the muscle, we can obtain the same results mentally and spiritually.

You are no bigger than what it takes to stop you.

Many even use religion as an escape. But you can't be a follower of Jesus Christ and use religion for escape. Jesus Christ was an ascetic in the truest sense. He didn't despise life; He *mastered* it.

*What did you mean,
"You can't legislate
morality?"*

You can't make people good by rules and regulations. Law and rules are necessary to bring order and protection to society. But we must not confuse restraint with transformation. Nor can we equate abstinence with goodness.

Many people who are restrained and legislated for 18 years at home come unglued when they go out on their own. There was really no loss of faith. They simply began to do what they had wanted to do all the time but didn't dare. Civilization may be nothing more than a thin veneer of restraint.

God's ultimate plan is to change our desires, not legislate our behavior.

What's the difference
between legal and
moral ?

Legal is *what* you do. Moral is *why* you do it. And we might add spiritual—for *whom* you do it. Immorality is also acute shortsightedness. The inability to see the big picture.

When a Negro lady decided to ride in the front of the bus it was illegal, but only she knew if it was moral or immoral. A wedding ceremony doesn't make sex moral—it does make it legal.

Abstaining from social no-nos doesn't make one moral. Too often morality gets credit for that which belongs to cold feet—or lack of opportunity!

what's the difference
between personality
and character?

Sometimes nothing. But it usually runs something like this: personality is what you parade on campus—character is what you are in the dark. For too many there is a great gap between the Saturday night date and the Sunday morning performance. Or between the public professions and the private practice.

What is the real test
of character?

Perhaps it can best be decided by your answer to this question. "What would you do if you could do it and knew you would never be found out?" If all the rules and regulations were taken away and you came unglued it might be concluded that you had no character. Character is determined by your desire to do what is best regardless of the circumstances or consequences.

You said, "If we ask what's wrong with something, we're off the track."

What's wrong with asking, "What's wrong?"

In the 12th chapter of Hebrews the writer compares life to running a race. With the race in mind he strongly urges us to "lay aside every weight."

What if you were going to run the hundred-yard dash and wanted to do your *best?* Would you choose to wear a pair of street shoes? Why not? What's wrong with street shoes? Do you see how the question of "right or wrong" is not the issue? Street shoes may be perfectly good, but not for a cinder track. In light of your goal, you simply lay aside the good thing that will keep you from doing your best.

Do you think you could pole-vault in a diver's suit? Anything wrong with a diver's suit? No. In fact, it would be just right if you were looking for sunken treasure.

More often than not, your question should be: "Is this best?" And that can only be determined by your understanding of God's plan for life in general and yours in particular.